TREASURES ON THE PAVEMENT
WRITTEN BY TOMMY WATKINS   ILLUSTRATED BY ASHTON MILLER

Garage sale day is the most popular day in the neighborhood.

Garage Sale

A girl listens to her favorite music while preparing to shop at the garage sales.

She rides her bicycle to all the households that have items for sale.

She finds items in each garage.

Dancing in the Dark

But she doesn't acquire the best item for the best price.

Finally, the perfect doll!

The doll is in good condition but overpriced.

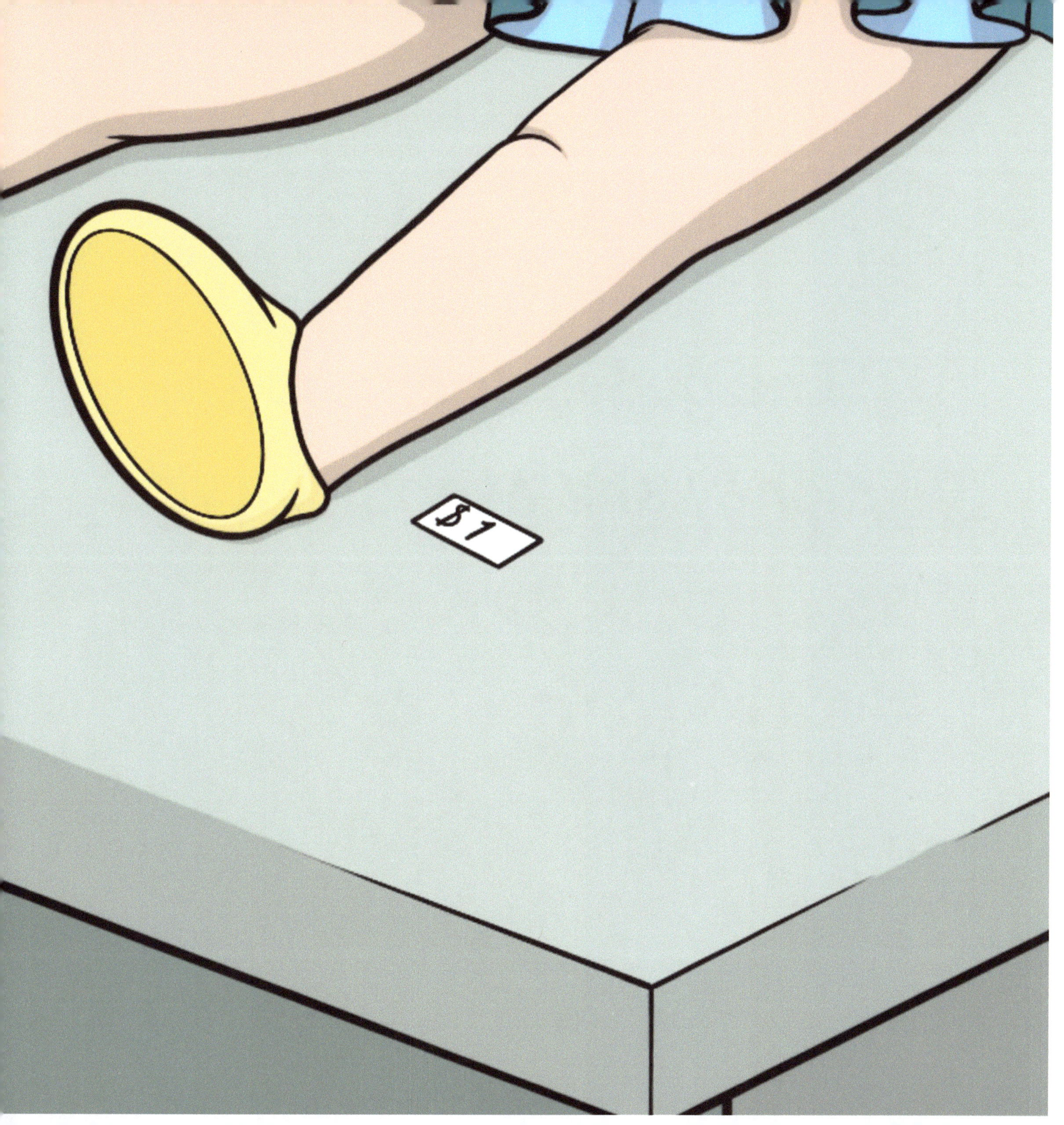

$1

The girl is short on the money she needs for the toy.

She walks up to the owner of the house and begins to barter.

"Excuse me, would you take 50 cents for the doll?" the girl asked.

"I was looking to get a dollar for the doll. I can sell it for 75 cents." said the man.

"My mother only gave me 50 cents. It is a beautiful doll." said the girl.

The man looks at the doll
and agrees to 50 cents.

"You have a deal." said the man.

The girl rides her bicycle home with her new doll.

Treasures can come from many different places.

Dancing in the Dark

Even from a garage.

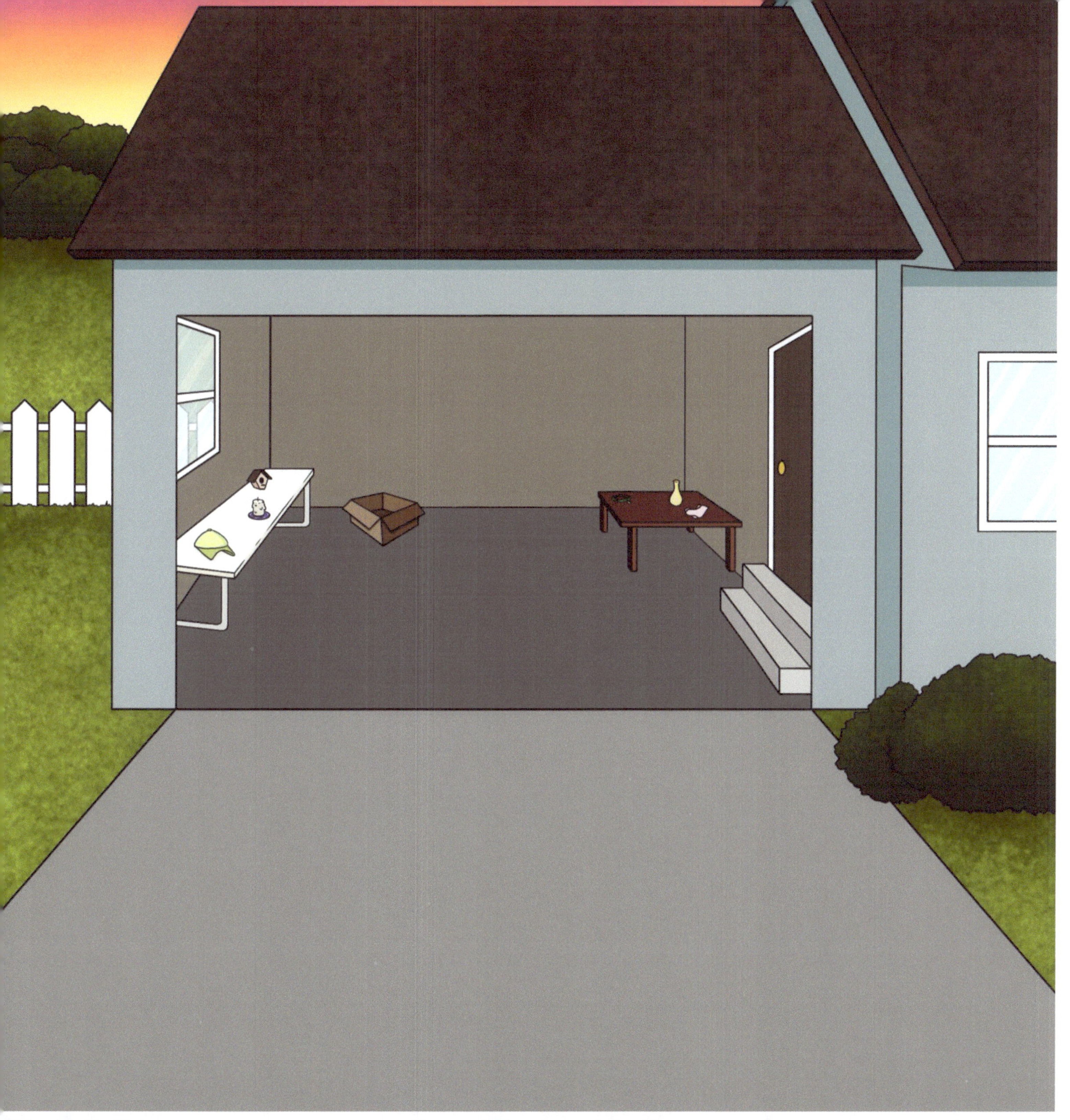

In a neighborhood on the pavement!

The End